I hope this finds you well

joanna michael

if you are reading this because you cannot sleep
haunted by the ghosts
wanting to believe in hope
then I wrote this for you

one of these poems is about you
I hope you find it

the molding

one

you would awaken me at night
beckoning me from the kitchen
and I would find myself at 3am
tippy-tip toeing, careful
not to awaken mother because I knew
she would be ashamed of me

and relentlessly,
you would demand I eat
until the cupboards
were as empty as I felt

two

the smooth, slick clay slid
between my fingers and I admired
how every movement caused a
ripple effect

the teacher says
do you understand?
the tiniest movements will
foreshadow its shape

thirty four

I would rather have you be
anorexic than bulimic
she would scream at me one day from the car

I am sorry I picked the wrong mental illness
I would silently plead, ashamed
from the passengers seat

three

you will cup your hipbones like
  handles on a trophy
play the victory song on the xylophone of your
protruding rib cage
and the anorexia will hiss:
this is the reason you have been starving

sometimes I think addiction makes
us feel like we are
flying
when we are
falling

two hundred & seven

at one point
I was so paper-thin
words left me
crumpled

one hundred & sixty three

he says
you can stop losing now
and I say *no actually*
I cannot and he says
what do you mean
and I say
I do not know how to stop and
when he does not say
anything else I realize
I have damaged more than
just my body

one hundred & eighty five

I awaken at night
and mother is standing beside my bed
watching me sleep, the house
is as desolate as
me

may I help you
I whisper and
we both laugh even though
it is not funny and
she says *I worry*
one of these nights
you will die and
I say *that is not*
going to happen

even though
I am starting to forget
how to stay alive

two hundred & twenty

my fear is I have pushed
people away for
so long that when
you finally touch me I will
shatter

one hundred

why do they teach us
the Pythagorean Theorem but
no one bothers to teach us
the equation for
self-love

[essay question]

one hundred & seventy nine

I spent hollow nights
gripping the steering wheel
with only the stars and God
to hear my sobs
my wails shall not be recounted

one hundred & forty four

she says
you look thin - are you sick? and
I do not know what to say so I
do not say anything and
then she points to her head and says
what I mean is, are you sick here

and then I know
someone understands so I say
yes

two hundred & ninety one

in one swift
sweeping motion I
clear out my closet
clothes that
fit a foreign, but healthy girl
seemingly hours ago
now drape on me like
curtains covering sunlight

I scoop up dresses and jeans
and red sweaters
dropping them in a box labeled
donation
mother scowls
disapprovingly from the doorway

I turn to face the closet
satisfied
it looks hollow and empty
like me

unnumbered haiku

and some days
it will be enough
to just be

one hundred & twenty nine

tell the hand to stop
the stomach yelled to the brain
and the brain said
the hand cannot hear me
because the demons are too loud

and I would find myself on autopilot
autonomously shoveling in food
my brain seemingly unaware
I was inching towards gastric rupture
which is fatal

eighty four

reach out to me and
take my hand
I do not know the way out
but I believe we can
find it together

[you are not alone]

two hundred & seventy five

what no one understands about
eating disorders is it has
nothing to do with food
and everything to do with
replacing emotional pain
with physical pain

one hundred & forty eight

I fantasize about food
like a lover I have yet to meet
in a dream, in a world where
we are together
undisturbed

fourteen

someday soon I
will be brave
climb the walls that
will not cave
defeat what says
I cannot be saved
untie the binds and run away

two hundred & eight

I never wanted to be thin
so much as I wanted to
control my pain

seventy eight

it was raining
the day you let me down gently
even the sky
mourned the ending of our story
even the sky
saw what we could have been

I exit while avoiding your eyes
afraid you are not hurting
afraid this was much
easier for you than it should be

I delicately, gingerly open
the latch on the gate because
I know mother does not expect me
home so soon
flatten myself against the stucco of the garage
will myself invisible
--- grateful I am invisible ---
and slowly peer around the corner

and through the rain,
I watch your car race to the end of the block

you cannot escape me fast enough
and your taillights are brilliant in the rain
burdenless

[and what scared me the most was change]

one hundred & ninety five

I am too quiet
because my mind
is too loud

two hundred & eighty

it is not that I was ever too fat
so much as the pain was
too heavy
one of us had to shrink

one hundred & seventy six

children
develop their own
relationships with food and their bodies
from everything you say
about yours

and if you speak negatively about any food
they will internalize it with shame
the next time they are offered
dessert

do not comment about
any body size ever
either positive or negative and
instead, compliment them on their
compassion, their
intelligence, their
talents, so they value these virtues over their
dress size

and always
be kind to your body
for you, for them

five

an eating disorder
is not always visible physically
but if you look closely enough
you will see
their eyes are always hungry

ten

of everything you can fear
a fear of yourself
is something I would not wish on anyone

I was the marionette and
the addiction was
the pupeteer

two hundred & eleven

the irony is
addiction will make you feel
both complete and empty
both comforted and lonely
bot free and restrained

maybe what makes you feel safe
the same thing
keeping you from change

[do not make your struggle your comfort zone]

one hundred & eighty seven

when you are anorexic you learn the difference
between a hug and a bone count

their fingers will sneakily trail along your
spine searching for any new vertebrae
threatening to betray your
secret

if you are smart you will learn to stand
pin straight and push back your shoulders
forcing every inch of skin to save you from
being thrown back into the hospital

I cannot hug you anymore
mother whispers to me one day before I leave
for school she says
it is too painful to feel

I did not argue because
I knew she was right

someday I hope I forget how lonely I felt
leaving libraries alone and shivering at
night in the dark

telling mother I was really out eating
dinner with friends
when in reality my only friends were in books

(the irony of a teenager
who lies to their parents
about being with friends
when she was really studying
was not lost on me)

but I will always remember
the day I made
my mother feel she needed to
stop hugging me

twenty four

an addiction is like a snowball
I shaped it and let it roll
downhill it traveled
I stood and watched it grow
and soon it was too big
for me to pick up and throw
I let it fester, let it breathe
then it was out of my control

nineteen

she waits outside in the cold.

it is spring, but the sun has not agreed with the time of year and snow still clings to the sidewalk. she is wearing a new, short skirt, although she cannot remember why, and her legs are spotted with goose bumps. she has been waiting for only a few minutes, she is actually early, but she is convinced he is not going to come. she wants to turn around and leave but she sees him soon enough. he walks up to her in only a few long strides by his long legs. she cannot help but smile. he greets her warmly. she cannot help but blush. he has a warm smile that made her feel safe in a way that became dangerous. he asks how she has been doing. she lies and tells him she is happy. she makes up stories about how excited she is for her future. without him.

they wait in line at the restaurant. there is a busy lunch crowd. everybody is there but nobody is there except the two of them. he knows what she is going to order before she orders it. they get to the front of the line; the lady at the counter asks if they are separate or together. she says separate. he says together. she looks at him, confused. the lady at the counter looks at him, bored. then he explains to them both; he says he will pay for her, if she wants. then she remembers he paid for her meal that Day He Let Her Down Gently, because he felt sorry for her. for what was about to come. and she was ignorant.

she asks him how he is doing. he says he is fine. is he really? she cannot tell. she wants to believe he is miserable; she wants to believe he misses her. she wants to ask if he has a new girlfriend, but she cannot because then he will ask if she has a new boyfriend and she will be too embarrassed to tell him no.

but he asks her, instead. he asks in a way that she cannot read. she cannot tell if he is asking just to be nice or if he really wants to know. she wants to believe he is jealous of the boyfriend who does not exist. he asks in a way that seems he is not sure if he wants the answer. *you got a boyfriend?* his voice is low.

she is surprised. she was not expecting him to ask. she is too embarrassed to say no. so she lies. she tells him yes. she tells him yes there is a boy. she says it is nothing serious, but yes, they have been casually dating. he says oh. that is all he says. she cannot tell how he feels. but she wants to believe his heart is breaking because her heart is breaking and now she cannot tell him the truth.

and then it is over. he hugs her warmly. she does not want to let go, but she knows now it is inevitable. when she does she walks away and he walks away and she knows they are not going back. they leave in separate directions.

unnumbered haiku

hunger pains
take my mind off of
other pain

[anorexia simplified]

one hundred & six

it sucked me under the current and
now I am out to sea
arms are flailing
                    see me waving?
                                        come rescue me

fifty seven

sometimes you came in a slow fade
and sometimes you whisked in seemingly
overnight
I waited each time for you to return
as I knew you would

like Alice, I was far too intrigued and enticed
by the rabbit, I overlooked the fact that I had
no idea
the scary place you would take me nor
how would I get back

and now I am trapped inside the looking glass
and you are the crystal barrier, the pretense
that distorts my perception
and I struggle and I fight, but I tire

but, you, darling, you are relentless.
I admire your energy, your fight, your drive
why am I not as strong as you?
you demanded favor
and I surrendered because
you were my comfort zone
and my trap at the same time

one hundred & ninety four

how thin must I get
before I look as hollow
as I feel

four

my heart thudded and purple spots danced
in front of my eyes
I am scared
I heard myself say from far away
but no one was around to hear

I braced my hands on the bathroom sink and
through blurry, watery eyes
I met the puffy-faced monster in the mirror
who was she? why was she so stupid?

I confessed to her
and to whatever other demons were lurking
in the bathroom with me that day:
I need help

two hundred & seventy one

if you are reading this
because you have
no choice but to be resilient
and need to believe
it gets easier sooner than later
I promise it does

the painting

twenty three

in the hollow 3am stillness
milky skin mimicking the moon
to the soundtrack of empty starving traffic
you will write a poem on my bare back with
your fingertips

[this is how we both will know]

one hundred & fifty three

I mixed colors of
our journey and
reluctantly colored
the vase

it is just going to go
through the fire
I protest
won't we be wasting
perfectly good paint?

not wasting
the teacher corrects
creating

two hundred & fifty nine

your hair and your eyes
and your smile and
the lines around it
made a new color

and I tried so hard
to think of what to name it

I did not even want to use it
to paint your memory
it was that invaluable

seventy five

someday you will see her smile and
you will forget how to breathe
at the same time, she will remind you
to keep living

hold on to her, please

ninety seven

the first time with you
was the last time with
someone new

[intimacy]

two hundred & fifty one

in another galaxy there are
scientists in a lab
on the verge of
powering cities and countries
with only a fraction of
our chemistry

and when we
cross paths
they will finally
have light

twenty nine

every night
her smile makes
the moon beam with envy

one hundred & twenty seven

you wrote your name
in goose bumps on
the inside of my forearm

one hundred & eight

the constellation
they have yet to name
is the stars in your eyes
burning holes through my pride

one hundred & forty six

and then
I saw you
and then
it all made sense

two hundred & ninety eight

I do not love you
the way I love sunsets
meaning I could stare at you for hours
fascinated (although
I certainly could)

I love you
the way I love breathing
it is purely inherent to my DNA

thirty nine

you will never know covet
until you see the way
they look at her

two hundred & eighteen

my favorite ways we said
I love you
were never with words

unnumbered haiku

I have loved you more
than some people will know love
their entire lives

eighty six

he looked at me
like I was art
he had only seen in a dream

two hundred

the first time
I saw his brown eyes meet the sunlight
felt like a smooth whiskey
melting brittle ice

one hundred & thirty three

I
remember the exact day
you made me forget

I do not remember
the exact day
I fell for
you

eighty two

in this negligent, volatile world
I am convinced we only
found each other by the light
of your smile

one hundred & nine

you made the most natural things
seem complicated
like taking my glasses off during the rain and
wiping the lenses on my shirt
hands fumbling, breath scattered

and you made the most complicated things
seem natural
as though these hands were only made
for the purpose of reaching for you
undone in the bed sheets

two hundred & forty nine

three cocktails deep he would confess :
it makes me crazy
he has no idea
how goddamn lucky he is

one hundred & twenty five

it does not matter how long you keep
two elements apart
when brought together
they will always have the same
reaction

[chemistry class]

one hundred & two

when he looked at me
I was filled with energy
that generated beauty

eight

and I said
show me where it hurts
and you
pointed to
the past

one hundred & sixty six

I want to be your support
when the storm rolls in
threatening your branches
I want to be the netting they place around you
to keep you from collapsing

I want to be your favorite sweater
you reach for when
the nights are their coldest and
I want to be
the first one you tell and
the last one who hears and
I want that to be exactly what you need

fifty one

kissing you
was like discovering
another sense

one hundred & twenty six

they were limbs interwoven in bed sheets
too dark for him to see
his own hand in front of his face but
her smile lit the way
guiding their hands to find each other

two hundred & four

I say
I do not want to
say goodbye and
he says *this is not*
goodbye and I say
you know what I mean

and when he does not
say anything I
know he knows
exactly what I mean

one hundred & ninety

our hearts
our hands
and our minds
will always be magnets

[they will always find their way back]

the shattering

fifty three

the night you left I stared into
the waves of the Atlantic
wondering how something could be
so calming, yet so tumultuous

seventeen

who are we as humans
to reduce something
as invaluable and
immeasurable as love

to something we should
fear

ninety

the vase slipped from my fingers and
running was all he could do
to save his feet from
being slivered
by the clay

one hundred & fifty one

the issue was
I chose to let a boy
hold my fragile self-worth
in his wavering hands
and called it healthy

[insecurity]

one hundred & ninety seven

I waited
too long for you
to not
be strong for you

unnumbered haiku

people have often
just turned out to be lessons
dressed as loyalty

one hundred & forty seven

why do we
throw the word love around
carelessly

as disposable as a water balloon
heaved at someone's shirt
it will sink into their skin and
rattle their bones

I do not say I love you
as loosely as you do, apparently
when I say I love you
I mean
I pray for your future
long after you decide
I am no longer welcome in it

one hundred & fifty seven

I lied when I told you I was okay
I was too proud to tell you
the same moon that used to
watch me beam
now watches me weep

unnumbered haiku

people do not change
who they are in one moment
they reveal themselves

sixteen

eyes like a lighthouse that searched the sea
I knew I was done when they stopped on me
let down my guard
I should have known better
she braided her hair before
she tied the tethers

the weatherman warned and
waved his red flag
but I pushed all the signs away
I was tied to the chair
by the time I heard the thunder
then all I could do was
watch my kingdom go under

forty three

the holidays have this irony where
you are constantly surrounded by crowds
but you are always lonely

one hundred & seventy five

she says
it is his loss as the
ice cream drips down her fingers the
sun is as hot as
a fever

she licks the ice cream
from the cone to save it from
being spoiled and I say
if it is his loss then why
do I feel so small and

she says *because*
you have condensed your self-worth
small enough to fit in the hands
of what was only temporary

maybe
he had to leave
in order for you to
expand

unnumbered haiku

you can be sitting
next to someone and somehow
still be missing them

one hundred & seventy two

be careful with who
you listen to
your favorite songs

two hundred & fifty three

maybe I am afraid
to open up because
what **comes** flooding out
may drown you

seventy two

you did not lose them
as though they were a set of keys
you cannot lose
what chose to leave

eleven

if mountains
are the result
of erupting volcanoes
you made a mountain out of me
and I do not know
whether to thank you
or to regret you

twenty

the absence of your answer
was the presence of your answer

[closure]

thirty three

the next time they
say they love you
I want you to ask them
what that means

two hundred & six

I wish that I could
purge you
as easily as
my dinner

unnumbered haiku

I only flinch now
when someone reaches for me
I have you to thank

two hundred & ten

and when you call me, sleepless and sobbing
and ask me why they left
I will tell you
because darkness hides from light

you have gifts they were not
prepared to open

two hundred & twenty one

I never said
we
would be easy

but I always believed
we
would be worth it

one hundred & eighty eight

this city is busy
and its lights are bright
and its crowds are loud
and with you
these used to compel me
but I now grumble
disapprovingly
I describe everything
in the same way
only now the words have
a bitter taste

twenty one

I am jealous of the moon now
she likes to gloat at me as she
gets to watch you smile
every night, your eyes
and the stars inside them light up at
who knows what and
even if she could tell me
I would still turn away in resentment
wanting to see for
myself

one hundred & thirteen

a broken heart
is a hangover you cure
by pouring another shot

one hundred & seventy three

if energy cannot be created nor destroyed
when we are, seemingly
strangers passing on the street
will we still be lighting up this city
with our chemistry?

thirteen

I sweep my closet and
remove everything that reminds me of him
I was left with a wardrobe as
hollow and abandoned
as I felt

one hundred & seventy eight

and now
you are everywhere
but you are nowhere

the rebuilding

sixty five

and I said
my garden is full of weeds
what should I do

and the universe said
now it is time to uproot

[we must tear down before rebuilding]

two hundred & seventy six

I recognize
want and need now

that boy I used to
cry for because I
wanted
was a sign that I
needed
self-assurance

two hundred & sixty six

you will always be
like autumn to me
everything was slowly dying but
too beautiful for us to notice

one hundred & sixty nine

validation
is a word for
giving someone
control of your
self-assuredness

eighty

my mistake was
using all my strength
trying to keep you
instead of using it to
fill the void
I should have filled first

I replaced a need for
owning my own
well-being with
a need for
falling in love

[accountability]

sixty six

what good is the vase now
he says as he
scoops the shattered pieces into
the trash

later when I am
alone I will
gingerly lift
broken piece after broken piece
from the chaos
gluing them together and
marvel, fascinated

one hundred & fifty five

here is what helped me: meet your self with empathy; meet your triggers with patience. do not give up. it is okay to isolate yourself from triggers. this is called cocooning. some people will understand. some people will not. it is okay to isolate yourself from them, too.

embrace anxiety. feel it. let it move. let it pass. do not give up. embrace people places and hobbies where you feel safe. do not give up. you will fall.

seek help. be resourceful. read books. read articles. talk with someone with whom you feel safe. this will instill accountability. if you do not have anyone with whom you feel safe, reach out to me. write your addiction a break up letter.

spend time with yourself. get to know yourself without your addiction. forgive yourself. you have interest and skills and desires you have not even crossed paths with because you have spent your time on this path with an addiction. and this is a beautiful realization.

above all I swear to you some nights will seem darker. some nights you will wonder if it is worth it and if you have even have a fighting chance. I swear to you that you do. you are reading this, aren't you?

do not give up.

Note: This is not intended to substitute professional medical advice, or to treat or diagnose any medical condition.

one hundred & sixty eight

your well being is
your responsibility and
maintaining this is
evolving

unnumbered haiku

I am no
longer afraid of
shattering

two hundred & forty eight

one thing I have learned
from the heartbreak

it has shown me
how much love I have had
surrounding me the entire time
I was too busy feeling sorry for myself
begging for his

[I am sorry I hurt you while I was hurting]

two hundred & fifteen

I am jealous of you
the sun cried to the moon
as brightly as I shine
they still only see you

the moon replied
with her hollow eyes
your light is so bold
they are afraid of being
exposed

one hundred & eighty nine

and when your heart is reaching for me
know that I am reaching for you too
and when you are
          missing sleep while missing me
just look up at the moon

twenty seven

the ghosts wake me up at night
to remind me
you are still gone

forty eight

everyone says
they are hurting
in a different way

[I am sorry I was not listening before]

fifty two

when someone asks me
what I am missing
I still feel your name
fester in my throat

unnumbered haiku

and your new girlfriend
should be thanking me right now
for your libido

[you are welcome]

two hundred & five

my attachment to you
was like snow
because pieces of you
began to slowly disappear
until one morning
I looked for you and you were

seventy three

I hope the moon
still reminds you of me
how I would beam at you
even throughout the wilderness

sixty nine

when we learn to write
we are taught
the best stories have
background, conflict and
resolution

and when I look in the mirror now
this all makes sense

one hundred & seventy four

I remember the days
I swore I would never get over you
stumbling into work
eyes swollen shut from crying
carrying you with me in the bags beneath them
I could not purge you fast enough

sometimes I drive by a coffee shop and
wonder if my ghost is still sitting there
defending you to the barista
I think I will let her be

as for me?

I have outgrown you

[growing pains]

one hundred & forty two

he says
you are doing it again and I say
doing what and he says
thinking you only have value if
a man can see it

and I purse my lips together and
try to think of an argument but
I know he is right

one hundred & sixty seven

I begged
for your love
because

I did not have it
to give myself

sixty three

I visit my grandmother's
solemn, humble grave
and tell her, tell the wind
about men I have tried to bribe to stay
with my loyalty

and from the graves around her
husbands argue, beneath fertile ground
love and control are synonymous

and I hear her tell me, tell the wind,
tell the flowers, tell the trees
tell the soil, because
finally somebody is listening:
you are much better off single
than with a love that drains you

and sometimes I hear the wives
in the graves around her
agree

two hundred & forty one

I am convinced
I will receive closure in the form of
you returning to say goodbye

but maybe I am not needing that
final piece of this puzzle
as much as I am needing to
put this puzzle aside and
begin a new one

fifty eight

if the last time we spoke was
the last time and
neither of us knew

maybe the universe has a different
idea of closure
than I do

seven

some girls
beg for attention

she takes yours
without asking

one hundred & ninety eight

I knew you were still
part of me when my heart
started pounding that day
in the park

before my eyes
even had a chance to know
you were close enough to
touch my
electrons did

two hundred & three

I replaced my need for
your approval with
a need for my own

[independence]

two hundred & ninety nine

I left you behind
in fragments
the way I lose
popcorn kernels in couch cushions

and one day I will
pull out pieces of you
wondering what else
is waiting to be
uncovered

one hundred & fifty eight

why do we tell a dog to heel
when we mean to follow?

when I heal
I would rather
let go

thirty seven

I have learned
to be vulnerable
is to welcome growth

one hundred & ninety nine

I release this
thing that has threatened to
destroy me
and its negative energy
like a boomerang

I cannot guarantee that
it will not come back but
I swear to you
I will
not stop
fighting it

you see
I have an eating disorder but
this eating disorder
does not have
me

one hundred & nineteen

her eyes
make you forget
to be cold

[melted]

sixty four

it is okay
to cry and
it is okay
to not cry

[therapy]

two hundred & fifty four

sometimes talking is like
energy leaving my body
through my tongue

[introverted]

fifty nine

the cancerous part kept me from breathing
like a vampire's heart it went on beating
pulled the plug and watched you die
wondered what was left inside

I packed up your remains and
carried you to the mortician's step
rang the bell twice and tried to forget
no one answered so I set you down
cold, crisp air, crunching fallen leaves on the ground

sometimes when I am lonely
I still walk by your grave
wonder if there was something I
could have done to have you saved

the wound still breathes from time to time
I worry your parasite will never leave my mind

eighty one

and to think
the stars in the sky
compete with
the stars in my eyes
when we both
look at you

two hundred & eighty two

if you are not whole
before them
you will only feel hollow
after them

[the night you left I felt vacant]

one hundred & thirty

loneliness is a word for time
you are given to spend with
this exquisite fascinating artful person
whose smile shames the moon and
whose eyes inspire the sunset

the ocean mimics your heart and
this is the same heart your
time alone should be spent
learning to appreciate

fifty

I have found
to forgive yourself
is to forgive who
first made you feel
inadequate

forty one

there are nights I still
look for the moon
to remind myself
we are not as far away
as it seems

[two solar systems]

two hundred & seventy seven

to tell you the
truth I could not
abandon you if I
tried I am just not
wired to desert people
and honestly I
love this about myself

twelve

when I feel lonely
I embrace the space
I have for
my goals

one hundred & seventy one

the day I moved to a new city
she said *let's go driving*

and when I asked
where we were going
she said *sometimes*
we have to get lost
in order to find
our way

seventy nine

he says
I do not understand
your compassion

and I think
that is how I know
you need mine

one hundred & thirty nine

the juvenile part of me
still wakes at night
wishing you are somewhere
lying awake in
regret

the self-assured part of me will
grip her shoulders
tightly, and shake them
the way mother did the night she
begged me to
save myself

do not wish their guilt
wish your freedom

two hundred & fifty six

and when I have shattered
you will find me unrecognizable
because all these cracks have
only made room
for my light to shine through

[the rebuilding]

the revealing

one hundred & twenty one

he says
I do not understand
how your heart is so big

and I think
because every time it breaks
it expands

thirty six

she says
what are you going to do
about the vase?
how do you plan to
fix its cracks?

and I say
what do you mean fix?
I plan to display them

two hundred & sixty three

you were not meant to settle
in this place where you cannot grow

the caterpillar can refuse to leave the cocoon
but eventually
it will outgrow its space and
fall

I would rather see you
fly

eighty seven

I am exhausted of this concept that
men are the only
abusers

[I have mistreated, too]

one hundred & five

other galaxies study earth
as this place where its inhabitants
treat love as a weapon
and they keep returning
puzzled

maybe that is why when people
die they never take the time to say
goodbye

their souls are saying
wherever I am headed next
I hope it is a place where
its people do not fear love

two hundred & thirty nine

if you lack love for yourself
you will not recognize unhealthy love
until it is too late

[boundaries]

seventy seven

I do not prefer we
fall in love
as though we are tumbling down a mountain
making a crash inevitable
finding ourselves
bloodied-knees and dizzied-heads
exploding on each other

I would rather we
evolve in love
as a piece of art forever unfinished
constantly adding colors of paint
we have yet to name
after artifacts from our journey

two hundred & forty six

everything given to you
is a loan

your hands must be
empty
before you can
receive
again

[yin and yang]

one hundred & sixty one

you have been looking in
the wrong mirror if
you cannot
see those wings

sixty eight

if I held up the vase
between us
how long would it take
for us to
see ourselves
in its reflection

one hundred & ninety two

I know you have convinced yourself
their love is the only love
that will make you feel whole

but if you had that same love for yourself
you would not have any need for
that person who cannot seem to
make up their mind about you

seventy one

what if babies are born crying
because they are now citizens of
this metallic, vapid, volatile
place we call earth, screaming
I had no say in this matter

just go
the universe tells them
and do the best you can to
not merely survive our earth
but to change it

ninety one

you are exhausted because
you are trying to forgive yourself
for what you had no control

[let go of what was never yours to carry]

unnumbered haiku

it is not too late
to decide your happiness
needs redirection

one hundred & sixty

if you continue to
view everyone through the filter
of your pain you will
find yourself decades from now
heart like an old bread heel
delicate yet hardened, refusing to soften

one hundred & three

healing is not
a checklist

it is
ongoing

[self-care]

forty six

we have internalized
a linear timeline of our lives
equals success

if we do not fulfill a
superficial milestone checklist
in precisely this order
at precisely the same age as our peers

if we skip a step or
repeat a step twice or maybe
move a few steps to a different age or even
add a few steps of our own then
we have somehow
failed

maybe the fact we are living beings
on this planet that revolves on its axis and
it revolves around the sun and the moon
revolves around it

maybe if the basis of our entire existence is
moving in a revolving non-linear fashion then
maybe our personal success is
allowed to as well

you have not failed
you have simply rearranged

[self-compassion]

eighty eight

you are most beautiful
in the moments you forget
to try

[authenticity]

two hundred & ninety five

what if we all had signs
on our hearts that read:
if you can read this you're getting too close

life would be so much simpler
if we knew when coming any closer
meant risking getting hurt

but then again
how many of us have driven right past
the warning sign
just for the adrenaline of seeing what was
on the other side

and if we could
live to tell about it

two hundred & seventeen

I wish I could tell you
the right thing to do
is to beg them to stay

but the right thing to do
is to let them go

and wait for what
the universe wants to give you next

one hundred & twenty three

do not let their toxicity
plant a home in
the tender soil of
that fragile soul of yours

twenty five

if the earth is constantly moving
do not think for a second
being complacent will keep you from
falling behind

there is no such thing as
staying in the same place

ninety six

if you get through the *I miss you* desert
and keep moving through the
what could I have done differently? forest
(although, I understand it is hard not to
set up camp there)

I promise you will build your home
in the land of
my best life does not depend on you

one hundred & ninety three

she went shopping
looking for her future
but her cart was too full
of the past

one hundred & sixty five

when I see you
lonely or bullied or abandoned
I see me

when I see you
begging for comfort
and sobbing out of loneliness
I see me

to be compassionate
is to see your reflection
in someone else

one hundred & one

she gets into her car and places the shade over the windshield. she wears her sunglasses; although they are broken, she refuses to give them up because they fit just right and the color looks just right and other reasons she does not remember but they were definitely good reasons. she starts the car and turns the volume up on her favorite songs. no, not that one. yes, that one. the one she listened to holding his hand while they were falling in love while they were falling asleep while they were falling somewhere neither one of them could see.

she presses on the accelerator. the shade is still on the windshield. she does not notice because she is without reason focused on the rearview mirror. as she drives, she spends her time making a list of all the things she would change. she cannot take her eyes off the rearview mirror and has no way of letting go.

she presses on the accelerator harder. she is really flying. good thing, too, because she has goals. the faster she drives the sooner she will get there. she has great ideas for what is going to happen in the future but every time she considers looking ahead that damn rearview mirror shows her something she just passed. it is too tempting to focus on the comfort of what is behind her instead of the uncertainty of what is ahead. if you were to ask why she insists on driving focused on the past she would say *it is important to recognize what went wrong so you will not repeat it in your future.* obviously. don't you know that?

and then there is the crash. it is as if everything is happening in slow motion. it is the most graceful, streamline, yet volatile explosion. she should be surprised but in some poetic irony it was almost as if she saw it coming. her head meets the windshield first and the glass shatters, unwittingly. she catapults through the windshield and rolls, almost in a perfect circular motion over the hood of the car and lands, every bone in her body giving way and crumbling into tiny pieces mixed with millions of shards of glass. she watches the glass shatter and sees the crystal light exploding on the ground. minute knives of glass stick out through her skin, her scalp, her bones, her heart. what did she even hit? she does not know and it does not matter because the shade was on the windshield and she was staring into the rearview mirror. she flies from the car and is thrown full-force into everything that lies ahead of her. the broken windshield designed to protect her is now reflecting what was destroying her.

she cannot cry for help and if she could it would not matter because everyone around her is staring behind them. her body, bloody, mangled, decapitated is now in an obscene manipulated position on the ground and no one bothers to raise an eyebrow to her. her head catapults from her body and rolls tumultuously on the ground, finally free of the body that refused to move forward.

it is all over. she is a head, resting, motionless on the side of the road. only now observing in what she is currently immersed. it is too bad all she can do is lay on the side and watch other cars fly past her; countless drivers staring into the rearview mirror, unaware of the danger in looking behind while moving forward. she wants to warn them, she really does, but she knows they will not be listening. they are too focused on what is behind them.

[learn to let go]

seventy six

growth is disguised as abandonment
it is often found in the wilderness
uncovered by resilience

one hundred & fifty

watch what comes out of
that smart mouth of yours because
your words have the power to
hurt or love or embrace or reject or belittle or
uphold
your future

two hundred & forty three

you board a bus
with your suitcase and
the bus stops at all the places
where you have been abandoned

you reach into the suitcase and
pull out everything that reminds you
of the pain
and throw it out the window

another woman will pick it up and
shove it into her suitcase

we are all
recycled pain

twenty six

like dolphins
the memories will resurface
gasping, reaching
only inhaling enough air
to survive

maybe the ghosts are here to remind you
learn from the past but
do not recycle it

ninety four

do not drop down your anchor
in the same ocean
that tried to drown you

two hundred & one

and it did not matter what she wore
as she was always wearing
her empathy

one hundred & thirty eight

the problem is not
how we self-medicate

the problem is we are not
helping each other heal

nine

there is a difference
between self care
and self medication

one hundred & twenty two

we were not meant to numb our pain
with addictions and social media
we were meant to heal
to grow, to become
compassionate works of art and
with vulnerability comes authenticity

ninety five

you have successfully
rebuilt yourself before when
you thought you would not stand again
now trust yourself that you will once more

[trust is a form of love]

thirty two

your body
has healed itself countless times
has walked from heartbreak
after those sleepless nights of you telling it
survival would be impossible
refusing to get out of bed
bemoaning life not working the way
you anticipated, your limbs
retaliated refusing apathy

and that heart kept beating, that brain
kept pulling at your bones, yelling
get up, get moving, we are not giving up here

do not war against what
fights for you

two hundred & twenty nine

if they choose to leave
do not beg them to stay

their needs simply did not line up
with yours and
they made the choice they felt was best for
their happiness

you can disagree with their decision
but you must respect it

it is much healthier
for you to live a life in
content
than
contempt

[you are not for everyone]

twenty two

embrace the difficult seasons because
the wilderness is where
you are brought closer together

[relationship]

one hundred & sixty four

hearts like yours are rare
do not expect them to understand

unnumbered haiku

to feel love again
you must first allow yourself
to feel through this pain

six

we are walking in the
mall and I see an
elderly man eating lunch
alone and he looks
like he has not ate
lunch with anyone in
so long his
silverware at home is
mismatched

I want to tell him
he is eating alone but
he is not alone so badly

she says something about a
sale at victoria's secret and
we are walking away as
those words fester and burn in my
throat and I go home and
ache for him this man

I cannot help but
see myself when
I see someone who looks
so alone they
are not even sure they are
still visible if they are still
tangible

fifty six

if they bully you
they are so
dark they need to
reduce those who
shine so bright they
are afraid of being
expelled they are
afraid of being
exposed

one hundred & eighty two

you are now holding my heart
and I do not wish to
remove your fingerprints

these words are
breathing
beating
bleeding
pulsing healing
into my veins

I wrote this for the both of us

one hundred & fifty six

your feelings
are validated
it is okay
to feel
hurt

but it
is not
okay
to hurt
yourself or
someone else

there is no justice in
recycling pain

two hundred & ninety

the people who say to
choose happiness are
lucky they can
make that choice

[mental illness]

two hundred & forty five

let yourself feel let yourself
cry lay on the floor
lay in bed all day
all week if you need to
pet the dog and
wait

wait it out wait
for it to pass because I swear to you
it will

[anxiety]

two hundred & fourteen

relationships do not work because
we put more trust in social media
than our partners

when did social media
become the criteria
for trust?

what happened to us?

one hundred & fifty two

there is no need to apologize for
choosing redirection
a candle cannot light another candle
without first being lit
and I do not mean pouring energy into
anything else
that further empties you
I mean fill yourself
with who you are
and do not ask for permission

unnumbered haiku

your intuition
is your childhood best friend
please don't ignore them

one hundred & forty three

sometimes we must forgive
before receiving an apology; it is
not for their well-being; it is
for your own

one hundred & forty

I still have nights
where I toss and turn
tangled in the bed sheets while
the voices scream at me
every second, of every hour
begging the sun to rise while
you sleep, your mind
quiet

and because I refuse to give in to the demons
consequently, I will spend the entire night
rolling around, restless
trying to drown out the voices by
staring at my phone as
minutes turn into hours and
then, when it seems as though
it will never come
the sun rises and
I have survived another night

this is my victory and
I know it is hard to believe
when the night is fog and
the moon refuses to beam but
I swear to you:

the light will come again

[recovery]

two hundred & fifty two

perspective is key

one hundred & six

she says *I am*
scared to move on and I say
we will not cross paths with
what is next if
we stay here and
ask why

it is not your job to
understand it is
your job to
trust

one hundred & thirty six

give yourself permission to
let go of today
so tomorrow can
have all of you

two hundred & twenty two

you cannot fully accept
what the universe has for you
in the next chapter
until you stop rereading the last one

sixty seven

I wish I knew what to say
to help with the pain
I am sorry you are hurting

the pain will not last forever
but the lesson will

eighty three

why do people say
my parents have been together for forty years
I do not know how they do it

I have not met your parents and
I know exactly how they do it
they do not fight *each other*
they fight *the problem*
they do it with the understanding that
giving up is not an option
why is that concept so lost on us?

they are business partners
you do not show up to work on the first day
then never come back
and expect to get paid
residually

you evolve as individuals, and as a unit
you set goals, trust, communicate, grow and

recycle forgiveness

forty four

experience ended class
by saying
your assignment
is to work on yourself

[growth]

sixty

this is our community:
you are safe in this space
safe from being belittled
safe from being judged
safe from being abandoned
you are understood

one hundred & seven

chase goals not people

ninety nine

in another galaxy
they are looking at you
in an art museum
calling you
masterpiece

[you have turned pain into art]

sixty two

how did I end up here?
he says, as I
watch him exhale
a drag into the
setting sun

it is all where you are going
I tell him
not where you came from

one hundred & four

trials take
energy that much
we cannot avoid but
what we can do is
control where the energy goes

let's put that energy
into being compassionates
not casualties into being advocates
not adversaries into being
healers not hurters into
growth not getting even
into being
stable not
stone

ninety three

you attached your tethers to their heart
and when they left they
ripped out the sutures
leaving you to bleed insecurity

do not build your foundation
in someone else
build within yourself first

two hundred & eighty six

maybe we have multiple soul mates
meaning each one is meant to give you
a few broken pieces
you will understand one day
we are all mismatched pieces of the vase
pieces they gave you and
        pieces you gave them in exchange
        pieces you no longer needed

you are much more eloquent and complex
than the one piece they gave you and
I am excited for you to see
the piece you will receive next

unnumbered haiku

few people will make
you forget to be bitter
please hold on to them

twenty eight

let's say you and me
start a new community
where we meet each other
with empathy
instead of pride
say we exchange compassion
instead of hurtful words we
lie awake regretting at night

say we abandon selfishness instead of
each other
and say when we feel
insecure we are *honest* with
one another

if our currency was empathy and
our cars were powered on compassion
what would it look like if
our lives were structured
in this fashion?

one hundred & thirty two

in this community
when you cannot stand
I will support you
because you
supported me when
I thought I would
crumble

[humility]

sixty one

you are always
closer to a miracle
than you think

eighteen

some days you will have to fight
those days will be the hardest
it will take everything in you to simply
get out of bed
put one foot in front of the other
and to keep doing so throughout the day

you will be exhausted and feel like
you have nothing left in you
before eight am

and you cannot tell anyone because
they will only say
you are doing great! and to
keep it up! but
no one tells you *how* to
keep it up
when it took everything in you to
make it to ten am
without your body
shattering on the floor

not to mention you will sit at your desk
and stare at words that
may as well be a foreign language because
the demons in your head are screaming so
loudly
you cannot concentrate on anything else and
God, it must have been at least six years by
now but
it is only noon

but you must keep fighting

[addiction]

one hundred & seventy seven

sometimes
closure is not
through answers

the resolution
is in not knowing

the growth is found
in what is left
unresolved

one hundred & fifty four

give to others
what was given to you
when you were too proud
to ask for it

[grace]

forty nine

the vase
now waits
to be filled again
not knowing
it is exactly that already

two hundred & thirty four

and in the end
what I once saw as
out of order
was only all
the pieces
falling into place

fifteen

when the ghosts
remind me of my
mistakes
I remind them
of my growth

one hundred & thirty seven

when the mirror boasts
a new wrinkle
I remember the vase

its cracks
boast light

thirty eight

I know you are
tired of hearing
this too will pass

so I will not tell you, again
and instead wait here
with you
to see it happen

[communion]

one hundred & eighty

you are a
multitude of presents
waiting to be
unwrapped

fifty four

call me when
you cannot sleep cause
the ghosts are too loud and
I will listen to them

unnumbered haiku

hearts are like walnuts
the toughest and hardest hearts
have the softest love

two hundred & sixteen

you are not responsible
for the happiness
of anyone else
but yourself

it is not your job
to make them happy

[boundaries]

one hundred & fifteen

the most
beautiful skies
come after
the most
difficult storms

unnumbered haiku

you must learn to meet
everyone with **empathy**
including yourself

8,002,738,255

if you have it in you
to give up

I am sure you have it in you
to keep going

I hope you read this in time

one hundred & forty nine

if we are all slowly dying
why aren't we all
constantly comforting

two hundred & two

your relationship should be
your refuge not
your cause

ninety two

the difference between
growth and bitterness is
life becomes less and less about
that thing that broke you
and more and more about
what you became from it

forty five

every season of your life
has something to be thankful for
and something to look forward to

two hundred & seventy three

we as humans
are water
living in vessels

we are drawn to
what
compels us

one hundred & ten

we are not
on a journey
to happiness

we are
on a journey
with happiness

one hundred & seventeen

you read this all the
way through
thank you for not giving
up on me
and I promise
to not give up on you

thirty

you have already met the love of your life

[read the first word]

one hundred & thirty five

I thumb the cracks
of the vase

gripping the handles
--- my hips ---
the mirror boasts each crack
--- each stretch mark each
wrinkle each
scar --- and
although I am not certain
which crack was produced
from which
fall
I am no longer
concerned with
analyzing

I am more interested in
revealing
a shattered vase is no longer
meant to suppress
but rather
support

I am no longer the
easel
I am the
art

forty two

yes
there are numbers missing

we leave behind what
we are no longer
meant to carry

[one to three hundred]

three hundred

someday, someone will pick up a vase
not that one! the universe will scream
that one has cracks
from where it has shattered

and they will lift the vase
to the light so that
the sun streams through
the broken pieces and they will say
that is what makes this one perfect

[you are the vase]

When Joanna Michael was in kindergarten, her teacher asked her mother to come in for a conference. Her mother quietly observed the classroom's art scotch taped on the wall as the teacher gestured toward one art project that stood out among the others it included a hand-written story in a hodge-podge of capital and lower case letters, written in bold crayon.

"That's nice," her mother smiled, politely. With no other children, she assumed all kindergartners progressed at the same pace. "You don't understand," the teacher objected. *"Five-year-olds don't write stories."*

Fast forward through a tumultuous love affair with eating disorders and a volatile journey to self-acceptance, the South Dakota native is currently a Denver resident studying mental health counseling. With an education in journalism, a handful of published magazine articles, she has always found prose as a form of therapy.

Her debut novel, a collection of prose entitled *I hope this finds you well,* will be a therapeutic collection geared toward the journey of emotional healing and self-love for those who have built homes in the wilderness of addiction, disordered-eating, and broken hearts.

joannamichael.com

Made in the USA
Coppell, TX
08 May 2021

55226430R00148